SAY

SOCIAL MEDIA

Simple Tips to
Help You Stay
Positively Connected

Chloe Ramsden

summersdale

SAY NO TO SOCIAL MEDIA

An Hachette UK Company
www.hachette.co.uk

Summersdale Publishers Ltd
Part of Octopus Publishing Group Limited
Carmelite House
50 Victoria Embankment
LONDON
EC4Y 0DZ
UK

www.summersdale.com

Printed and bound in China

ISBN: 978-1-78783-539-9

Substantial discounts on bulk quantities of Summersdale books are available to corporations, professional associations and other organizations. For details contact general enquiries: telephone: +44 (0) 1243 771107 or email: enquiries@summersdale.com

Disclaimer
All information correct at time of printing.

CONTENTS

INTRODUCTION

The past 20 years have seen a revolution. Social media has transformed every aspect of our lives – from how we take photos and stay in touch to how we talk about and consider our mental health.

Our vocabulary now includes terms such as "selfie", "share", "hashtag" and "influencer"; we have social media celebrities; we "follow" complete strangers; and no detail is too personal or intimate to be posted on our feeds.

The boom has come hand in hand with the smartphone explosion, as the compulsion to check our phones is quickly followed by the desire to check social media. The result is that we now spend a seventh of our waking lives on social media such as Facebook, Instagram, Twitter, Snapchat, Pinterest and TikTok.

But it's a double-edged sword. Full of discovery, entertainment and information on one hand, social media can cause self-criticism, a loss of focus and concentration and loneliness on the other. Meanwhile, there is mounting evidence that it is linked to anxiety and depression, not to mention the stress that arises from trolling and online bullying.

These are serious issues considering that some 3.48 billion people are on social media – that's 45 per cent of the total world population.

It's time to take control over your social media habit – and stay in control. This book is packed with tips and easy steps for setting rules and creating a healthy relationship with social media. The end goal is for you to enjoy a functional social media habit, in which you are very much in charge.

KEY

	Tips to help you check in with yourself and think about things in a different way
	Tips that reduce the time you spend on your phone
	Tips that focus on your mental well-being
	Something new to try that can be implemented right away
	Options for those who have mastered the basics

Social media relies on "brain hacking", a term that describes the way it exploits the brain's reward system to keep us coming back with the promise of instant gratification (i.e. more likes on Facebook, Instagram and Twitter, and streaks on Snapchat).

Using Facebook can make people feel worse. In a 2014 study, participants reported lower moods after going on Facebook for 20 minutes compared with those participants who merely browsed the internet. The Austrian study suggested that people's moods were negatively affected because they saw it as a waste of time.

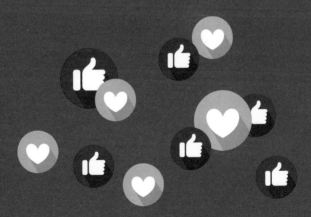

"Social media addiction" has been referred to in a wide variety of studies and is thought to affect 5 per cent of young people. Some view it as potentially more addictive than cigarettes and alcohol.

SOCIAL MEDIA COULD BE AFFECTING OUR SELF-ESTEEM AND BODY IMAGE. NEARLY HALF OF 18–34-YEAR-OLDS REPORTED THAT SOCIAL MEDIA MAKES THEM FEEL UNATTRACTIVE IN A SURVEY OF 1,500 PEOPLE BY UK DISABILITY EQUALITY CHARITY SCOPE. RESEARCH HAS ALSO FOUND THAT WOMEN COMPARE THEMSELVES NEGATIVELY TO SELFIES OF OTHER WOMEN WHILE ADOLESCENT GIRLS WHO SHARE MORE SELFIES ONLINE AND USE MORE PHOTOSHOP FEEL WORSE ABOUT THEIR APPEARANCE.

Feelings of anxiety or envy from what we see
on our feeds before bedtime keep the brain on
high alert, preventing us from falling asleep,
while the light from devices can suppress the
release of the sleep hormone melatonin.

The University of Copenhagen found that quitting Facebook, even for a week, made users feel more content, rating their well-being as higher as they escaped the trap of "Facebook envy" – thinking other people's lives looked better than their own.

Social media can heighten anxiety by increasing users' ability to keep up to date with the activities of their social circles.

FOMO (fear of missing out) has been linked to intensive social media use and is associated with lower mood and life satisfaction.

Social media can affect young people the most. Nearly half of all girls in the UK (aged between 11 and 18) have suffered some form of abuse or harassment on social media, while 40 per cent of boys have experienced online harassment.

Social media knows more about you than you think. Everything you do on Facebook is stored, from every single time you've logged in to Facebook, the location you logged in from, what time and from what device, to all the applications you've ever connected to your Facebook account, not to mention every file, sticker and message you've ever sent.

USE OF SO-CALLED "SOCIAL" MEDIA HAS BEEN
SHOWN TO CORRELATE WITH LONELINESS, WITH
MORE TIME SPENT ON THE MOST COMMONLY
USED SOCIAL NETWORKS LINKED TO HIGHER
FEELINGS OF ISOLATION AND ANXIETY.

WHERE TO START

By picking up this book, you've taken the first step in changing your relationship with social media. So what's next? Don't worry, you don't have to quit overnight – it's enough to start by making a few small changes, which is the best way to form lasting habits. Here are a few methods and techniques for taking the next steps to overcoming your social media cravings.

1

PAY ATTENTION

The first real step to changing your relationship with social media is to pay attention to your habits. You need to gather data on your behaviour. A study looking into how people feel after using Facebook found that the participants always thought they'd feel better afterward, but in actuality they felt worse.

So, first, observe your reactions: how do you feel when your phone beeps or vibrates? What emotions do you feel when you first tap on one of your feeds? And what are your emotions and energy levels like when you finally leave your feeds? Keep a diary. Logging those facts and observations about your social media habits will create a solid foundation for creating positive new ones.

2

GO ON A DIGITAL DIET

How would you feel if you ate junk food all day? Lethargic and possibly possessed with a queasy mixture of guilt and the desire for more? Compare that to a day of balanced eating, in which you've consumed fruit and vegetables, healthy protein, whole grains – even with a treat or two thrown in. Social media is junk food: cheap, instantly tasty and satisfying, but with few long-term benefits. You wouldn't eat burgers, fried chicken, deep pan pizza and chips every day and expect to feel good. The same applies to social media – think about how time away from your feeds could make you feel. You'd be energized, your brain would be less foggy and you'd have the get-up-and-go for real mood- and body-boosting activities.

3

TRACK YOUR USAGE

How much time do you think you spend on social media? Write down the hours and minutes that you imagine you lose to your feeds. And how many times do you jump on Facebook, Instagram, Twitter and your other accounts per day? Take a guess and write it down. Now download a tracking app on your phone to find out the real figures. There's no shortage of apps but popular options for iPhone and Android include Moment, Offtime and RescueTime.

4

CHECK IN WITH YOURSELF

Before you go on your phone, ask yourself why and what you want to achieve. Checking your feeds can be prompted by notifications, messages and likes that you may want to respond to. You might be passing the time on your commute, in the waiting room at the doctor's or in a queue. Perhaps your Facebook and Twitter accounts keep you updated on current events. Or is it a form of comfort? Work has stalled, you've had an argument with someone, you're bored, upset or lonely. It's important to understand the reasons behind your social media habits. To help you notice how often you're checking it, put a rubber band around your phone or stick a Post-it note on to the screen, which will stop you unlocking your phone on autopilot.

5

TELL YOUR FRIENDS

It's all very well thinking about changing habits and imagining a day when you might give up social media. But if you want to make changes now, you need to spread the news. Let your friends and family know that you are trying to control your social media habits. Just announcing it will make it feel more real. Tell them what your plans are – experts say that encouragement from friends, colleagues and loved ones provides the accountability and necessary support for successfully achieving goals. They can keep you on track and provide reminders – and enthusiasm – if your mission starts to waver.

6

PICTURE IT

Visualize what you will gain once you've got your social media use under control. Rather than seeing this as a loss, think positively about the outcome. You have so much to gain: free time, better sleep, a re-energized focus, and perhaps you'll get through that stack of books you've been meaning to read! To really make a change, we need reasons, motivation and incentives – visualization will help you remember why you're tackling your social media usage.

7

BUDDY UP

We've talked about telling other people about your plan – now get them on board. Recruit a friend to join you. You'll be able to discuss your experiences together and knowing that someone else is doing this with you will spur you on. A friend will also keep you accountable: it can be easy to go back on commitments that you've made to yourself, but it's harder to let someone else down. Give your buddy permission to call you out if you fall off the wagon (for instance: if you find yourself pulled into an hour or two of scrolling). And don't forget that the people who know you best might have helpful ideas about what works for you that you can't see yourself.

8

START SMALL

Make small, manageable changes and enjoy the feeling of success. For instance, you might commit to making your bedroom a social-media-free zone for one day a week. Or give yourself an afternoon when you won't "like" anyone's posts in order to see how that feels, or try watching a half-hour TV show without delving into your feeds to see what other viewers are saying. Making drastic changes too early in your journey may sabotage your progress, as they'll be harder to maintain. Instead start by choosing achievable tweaks to your social media routines, and you will soon build confidence in yourself.

CREATE BARRIERS

Make checking social media just a little harder than usual. One of the aspects of social media that makes it so hard to stop is the sheer ease of access – a few taps and you're sucked in. So if you're brave enough, delete the apps on your phone so you can only check your feeds on your web browser (this is not irreversible). Or simply pledge to spend time on Instagram, Facebook, Twitter and the like on your phone's browser. The browser versions are clunkier and less appealing than the app versions and may prompt you to question why you're on the sites at all.

10

FORGIVE YOURSELF

It's inevitable when making any changes that we will slip up or give in to temptation sometimes. It's natural to beat yourself up if you seem to fall down a social media rabbit hole, or to blame yourself for "ruining" the experiment. Self-compassion is key here. Remind yourself that it's a brief lapse and it doesn't undo all your good work. Ask yourself what you would say to your buddy if they slipped up on their social media project. Don't speak to yourself any more harshly than you would to your friend. And remember: tomorrow is a new day.

TAKE BACK CONTROL

You have set the stage to start making real changes to your social media use. Now it's time to flex your social media muscles, but don't worry – you are stronger than you think. Follow these tips to slowly but surely gain control over your social media. With a few easy steps, visiting your feeds will feel like a positive choice rather than a mindless habit. Here's how to get started.

11

SET TIME LIMITS

We're all used to the feeling of checking Instagram for "two minutes" only to emerge an hour later. Good news: you have the power to control the amount of time you spend on your feeds. Start by setting your phone alarm. Perhaps you'll give yourself 30 minutes a session, or you might prefer to keep a tighter leash on yourself and choose just 10 minutes per go. The amount of time is up to you – this exercise is about making deliberate choices with social media rather than being sucked in by it.

12

CLEAR THE CLUTTER

Cult clutter-clearer Marie Kondo exhorts her admirers to chuck out anything in their homes that doesn't spark joy. The same is true of your phone and laptop. Delete the apps that exhaust your time and energy, and that make you feel bad. This exercise is about reframing your relationship with your devices to make them sources of positivity, not of toxic feelings. Is there an app for a gym that you never go to? Hit delete. Does the app drain your battery? Delete. And ask yourself when you last used it. If it was a year ago – delete.

13

REFRESH YOUR DISPLAY

Rearrange your apps so only the most important and useful ones are on your home screen: maps, the weather, the clock, banking, the calculator and notes. Now move all social media apps to page two or even three of your home screen. Go one step further and hide them in folders to make accessing them just that bit harder. To add another obstacle, try putting the apps in folders with names that are completely unrelated to the apps in question. Do the same on your computer, removing social media accounts from your bookmarks and toolbar.

14

LOG IN MANUALLY

Don't save your logins on your apps. Visiting your feeds has been made extremely easy, so *you* will have to make it harder. Change your phone or browser settings so they don't store the passwords to your accounts. Then rather than simply closing your browser or swiping the app away when you're finished, you have to log out. It's cumbersome and fiddly – and that's the point. Suddenly social media involves a bit of effort.

15

CHOOSE NO NOTIFICATIONS

Who among us isn't familiar with the dog-whistle sensation of our phones buzzing and pinging with every new notification? Those notifications are prompted by every "like" and comment on Instagram and Facebook, and any message – no matter how inconsequential – on WhatsApp. The constant buzzing and ringing makes you feel distracted and keeps you on constant high alert. But there's an easy fix: turn off push notifications and bask in the new-found peace and quiet. If you want to check for new likes and messages, you will now have to visit the app itself.

16

GO QUIET

You've turned off notifications, but are you still spending your days with a chorus of pings, rings and alerts as messages and emails come through? Each noise will prompt a subconscious response: the desire to pick up your phone. And, of course, from picking up your phone it's a seamless motion to tapping on a social media app to check what's new. The solution? Turn your phone to silent and take off the vibration feature. Now you, not your phone, are in charge of when you look at social media.

17

GO GREY

Social media is full of colour – just think of Pinterest and its endless images of dream interiors, Snapchat's bright filters, and the photos and memes that fill Twitter, Facebook and Instagram. Both Apple and Android phones can be set to a greyscale screen – this will strip the colour from all displays, turning your device and all its contents an unappealing black and white. Without the different shades to make your app icons and messages "pop", the images on the screen stand out far less.

18

WAKE UP!

Buy an alarm clock. Choose an old-fashioned one that rings or beeps at the allotted time, or opt for a radio alarm that will bring you round with music or talk radio. There are also light-based alarms that gradually lighten the room so you wake up in "daylight". Whatever you go for, this clock will replace your phone alarm. There's logic to this: if your phone isn't in your bedroom or on your bedside table it won't be the first thing you pick up in the morning, sucking you in during those precious first minutes of the day.

19

SCHEDULE TIME OFF

Try scheduling internet-free time. You will be creating moments of peace, maybe even of boredom, to let your mind wander and notice the world around you rather than your phone. Start by giving yourself a 5-minute pause between waking up and picking up your phone. Once you've done that, schedule longer periods of downtime: an hour before bedtime, or between 8 p.m. and 8 a.m. You could block out the busiest hours in the morning so you're fully focused on your studies or work. How does it feel? Which phone-free times felt the best or were the most productive? If you need extra support, app-blocking programmes such as Freedom, or BlockSite, a Chrome extension that won't let you access sites of your choice, will help.

20

NO-PHONE ZONES

Start by creating device-free zones. As well as banning your phone from your bedroom, make your sitting room a no-phone zone for an hour in the evening and practise watching TV without it to hand. Commit to leaving your phone outside the room during mealtimes so you can be 100 per cent focused on the food you're eating and the conversation with your family or housemates. When you're eating out with friends, put your phone away during the meal. How does it feel to enjoy the moment?

FIGHT FOMO

One of the toughest aspects of social media to overcome is the sense that life is going on without you – that when you're not online, an endless parade of photos, comments, discussions, chats and in-jokes are all taking place but you're not involved. Not to mention that sinking feeling when you see photos and videos of events that you weren't at. Here are some fail-safe techniques to help you conquer your fear of missing out.

21

IT'S A HIGHLIGHT REEL

Remember that social media is a highlight reel. Most feeds do not accurately represent people's real lives. They don't spend every day at a spa, on the slopes, or lounging on a tropical beach – and that's why they're posting those images. The moments that we choose to capture on social media are designed to make our lives look better, more fun and glamorous than they really are. Social media is a reflection of who we want to be rather than who we really are. So, that FOMO you're feeling? You're comparing yourself to someone else's online persona. When you see images that give you that envious, frustrated FOMO feeling, tell yourself: "This isn't real."

22

YOU CAN'T BE EVERYWHERE

It's a certain kind of torture seeing posts from friends at a dinner, party, drinks, exhibition or a gig and not being there. But you can't be everywhere all the time. Take a moment to remember where you were at the same time – were you out having fun somewhere else? Or perhaps you were at home relaxing and watching Netflix or reading a book. And what's wrong with that? On a piece of paper, write down the social media post that prompted these negative emotions and write down next to it why you weren't there. Think very honestly about what you were doing and note why you chose to do it and whether you enjoyed it. Putting it down in black and white will help remind you that you made a choice, and it was the best choice you could have made at that time.

23

GRATITUDE ATTITUDE

Research has found that the more someone is inclined to gratitude, the less likely they are to be depressed, anxious, lonely or envious. So instead of focusing on what you're missing out on, think about everything you're grateful for. Take a page in your diary or a notebook and write a gratitude list. As well as the central, important figures and essentials in your life – such as family, friends, pets, a roof over your head – jot down the habits and benefits you might take for granted: a fridge full of food, enjoying a cup of tea in bed or a daily hot shower. Your list is entirely individual to you, and nothing is too big or too small to be grateful for. Simply writing this list will make you focus on how much you already have.

24

WHAT TO DO WHEN FOMO STRIKES?

When you notice your thoughts leading you into a FOMO spiral, consciously take a couple of minutes to relax your body. Stop, breathe and become aware of your surroundings and how your body feels. Scan it for any tension and relax any muscles that you're unwittingly tensing. Breathe in and exhale slowly as you think of a special memory or a favourite place. Keep inhaling and exhaling slowly as needed. This exercise can reduce stress and anxiety, and boost your mood.

25

REMEMBER IT'S NOT REAL

As the novelist Erica Jong once said, "Jealousy is all the fun you think they had." That photo of your friend beaming at a party you didn't go to? Perhaps she had a miserable night and didn't speak to anyone, but plastered on a smile for that one picture. That influencer posing on holiday in an impossibly beautiful location? Perhaps she and her boyfriend have been arguing since the plane took off? And the photo of an acquaintance posing by the pool – you aren't to know that she only posted the twentieth shot because she didn't like the other nineteen. Repeat after me: social media is not reality.

26

ENJOY MORE ME TIME

Give yourself permission to have some "me time" and recharge in your own way. This will differ from person to person – perhaps you like to watch films in your pyjamas, walk your dog, read a trashy novel, tackle a craft project or even plough through some personal admin? Whether you plan your me time for the day or night, don't worry about what you think you *should* be doing. Staying in and deliberately giving *yourself* – not your phone – some attention is good for you and will help you lose that FOMO feeling.

27

TRY BEING LOGICAL

When we're hit with a burst of negative – and sometimes irrational – emotion, it can be helpful to work through it by thinking logically. Let's say you've seen a photo of a group of friends hanging out together on social media. You might instantly feel upset that you weren't included, but ask yourself if there is a good reason that you didn't get an invite. How close are you to the event organizers – would you really have expected an invitation from them? Was it a very spontaneous get-together? Or are there other factors at play – for instance, did this gathering take place in another location, away from your home town? If you think about it, you may realize that there's a perfectly good reason that you weren't part of the gathering. Write a positive comment under the photo and move on.

28

TURN FOMO UPSIDE DOWN

Try reframing your FOMO. You might be filled with stress and anxiety as you scroll through your feeds, spotting parties, nights out, holidays and dinners that are going on without you. But this sheer act of scrolling, spending your precious time feeling resentful and jittery at other people's lives, takes away from *your* life. Think about what you're missing out on in the real world when you're on social media. You could be sitting on the sofa with your loved ones when you're locked into your feeds but they may as well be somewhere else for all that you're noticing them. Think of it this way: missing out on social media is a good thing.

29

SCHEDULE TIME TO CHECK

Take practical steps to limit your FOMO. If you're at the point that you are able to step away from your phone for long periods of time – let's say during the workday, or from late evening to early morning – you might be worried about missing out on invitations sent through social media. Make a point of checking your accounts from your desktop computer or laptop once or twice a day, but once you've glanced at your notifications and messages then log out until you're next scheduled to go back on social media.

EMBRACE JOMO

You've realized what your FOMO is really about, and by now you should be able to stay off social media for sustained periods without that niggling feeling of life happening without you. A whirl of posting, liking and messaging is no substitute for true human connection, so now is the time to embrace the real, tangible world around you and gain precious, nourishing experiences with the people you love offline. Are you ready to make some memories? Here are some tips to help you love and incorporate JOMO – the *joy* of missing out – into your life.

30

LEARN WHAT YOU LOVE

If you're on social media less then you've gained more free time. If you don't know what to do with this free time, you may feel at a loose end, listless or anxious, and there is a danger that you'll relieve these uncomfortable feelings with the mindless distraction of social media. Don't do it! Instead, get back in touch with what makes you happy in your offline life. Write a list of activities you have always wanted to do and of what you used to do before social media dominated your free time. Plan a walk with a friend, get baking, go for a swim – there is so much fun to be had!

31

GO SOLO

Loneliness is often the reason people spend time on social media, only to find that it makes them feel more socially isolated. A study from the University of Pittsburgh and West Virginia University found that positive experiences on social media may be linked with a quick hit of positive reinforcement, but negative experiences – such as public social media arguments – can leave a lasting, upsetting impression. Instead of seeking fulfilment from the online world, learn to enjoy your own company and the wonderful freedom of being alone. The first few times you do something on your own it may be frightening and overwhelming but then as you make it a habit, it becomes natural – just like reaching for your phone. Reframe your solo time offline – it's a choice and you're investing in *you*.

32

GO ON A "ME" DATE

The more you enjoy your own company, the more you will be able to resist the lure of your feeds to distract you or give you a fleeting sense of validation. Practise independence and self-sufficiency by going on a date with yourself. Take yourself to the cinema – try a matinee or midweek evening showing if you feel self-conscious on a Friday night. Sit in a cafe, order your drink and savour it with a book, crossword or people-watching – letting your brain wander. If you feel uncomfortable or anxious, ask yourself why. Think about your feelings instead of smothering them with mindless social scrolling. Sit with your discomfort and it will soon pass.

33

GO FOR A WALK

This is such a simple activity but it's rewarding. You might be used to checking Instagram as you stroll, or catching up with friends on Facebook Messenger, or sending photos of the beauty around you to a WhatsApp group. Instead, try walking without "plugging in". Pay attention to the streets or paths you're walking on. What's the weather like? How does it feel to be wherever you are? Listen to your breathing, and feel the rhythm of your feet as you take each step. If you're on a street, observe the people around you. If you're in nature, let your eyes rest on that far horizon – the soothing opposite of being lit up by a blue-light-emitting screen.

34

GET PHYSICAL

Can you think of any physical benefits to spending time on social media? Your head is bowed, your shoulders slumped toward the screen, while the only motion in your body is in your fingers. Doing something active boosts mood, your sense of well-being and the brain's functioning. Do yoga, take a dance class, get a massage, or even try sitting on a medicine ball instead of a chair at home. These activities will help you connect with your physical self again, and remind you of the joy of moving your whole body – not just fingers and thumbs across your screens.

35

BOOST YOUR IQ

Time off social media may make you more intelligent. The brain is said to have two kinds of attention: spotlight and floodlight. When you're focused on a single task, the spotlight brain is focused on completion – that's the feeling of "flow" that you experience when you're immersed in something. But when our concentration is split between several tasks – checking emails, jumping on Instagram and Facebook, all while writing a report – the brain uses a floodlight approach. University of London researchers have found that computer-based multitasking decreases IQ more than smoking marijuana or losing a night's sleep. So tackle tasks one at a time, and once the job at hand is finished you can treat yourself to a short session on social media.

36

IMPROVE YOUR ATTENTION SPAN

Neuroplasticity is the process that occurs when the brain forms new connections in response to new situations or changes in the environment. Many things can change the brain, such as learning a new language, meditating and listening to music. Social media can also have an impact. A Microsoft study found that human attention spans reduced from 12 seconds in 2000 to 8 seconds in 2013. If you're very dependent on your device and its feeds, you may struggle to focus on anything for very long. But you can get your attention span back. Try simple mental maths, put on a song and listen to the lyrics, or read a book (although avoid reading a Kindle if possible – printed books give the brain a better workout, increasing critical thinking and boosting your ability to absorb the details).

MEDITATE

Meditating is the opposite of being on social media. Rather than flitting from platform to platform, images, videos and words whizzing past your eyes with flashes of colour, meditating is a time of stillness and focus. It's about emptying your mind, listening to your breath and just letting yourself "be". The extra free time you gain by taking control over social media is a gift to yourself that you can't ignore. Sit down for 5 minutes (set an alarm), close your eyes and focus on your breathing. If you are struggling to concentrate, the Headspace app offers bite-sized guided meditations that will fit into anyone's schedule.

38

GIVE YOURSELF A GOAL

Is there a goal you'd like to reach in your studies or career? Logging off from social media gives you a chance to devote your full attention to these areas of your life. Take the opportunity to set a target for yourself and work toward it, using your social media downtime to focus on this project. With your increased focus, without being pulled away into online worlds and distracted by events going on wherever you're not, you will find a new sense of enjoyment and satisfaction. Real engagement in a task is highly rewarding and will give you a true sense of your aptitude. It will also show your bosses or teachers what you're made of.

39

GO SLOW

As with other "slow" movements (such as slow food and slow TV), savour the peaceful moments you can find when you aren't plugged into the hubbub of social media. JOMO is being able to proudly admit that you're embracing a slower pace of life, and that you're self-confident enough to consciously take a step back from your feeds. By unshackling yourself from social media, where information, conversations and life move at breakneck speed, you can operate at your own pace. Instead of thinking about what you apparently *should* be doing, you'll be thinking about what you *want* to do – at a schedule dictated by you.

ACCEPT YOURSELF

A central part of social media's appeal is the apparent validation it gives. But the buzz of having a selfie liked can turn into a feeling of depression and anxiety if another photo doesn't get the same reaction. Meanwhile, filters and photo-editing apps can erode self-confidence in your natural appearance. Now it's time for you to tackle those insecurities, get in touch with the real you and learn to love yourself for who you really are.

40

TALK TO THE MIRROR

What positive comments do you most need to hear? Perhaps you don't think you're as witty as your friends, or you're not satisfied with your looks – especially compared with other people on social media. Write a list of phrases – they can be anything from "I am funny" to "I am myself, I am unique, I am beautiful." Choose a time each day to recite them to yourself. Look in the mirror and, using a confident voice, slowly repeat these phrases. If you repeat them every day you may even help replace those old default negative thoughts with these new positive ones.

41

COLLECT COMPLIMENTS

Whenever anyone gives you praise or makes a positive comment about any aspect of your personality, work or achievements, write it down on a piece of paper. Create a "compliment box" filled with these comments and revisit them when you're feeling low or a bit wobbly. Don't doubt them either – these are compliments from people who know you, care for you and see your true self.

42

KEEP A DIARY

Being on social media involves a lot of passive consuming, whether it's edited snippets of other people's lives or information, videos and pictures posted by people you barely know – if at all. Instead of being an expert on the lives of strangers, do something that will help you to learn more about yourself. Journaling is a good way to start – write every day, as little or as much as you like. You won't have an audience, so you won't be influenced by the pressure to entertain your social media followers. Think for yourself, and discover your real voice. Each entry will take you closer to understanding yourself better.

43

BE YOUR OWN CHEERLEADER

Social media can wreak havoc on our self-esteem, whether it's a nagging worry that your captions aren't quite funny or clever enough or envy that a pal has more followers and posts better pictures than you. So pay attention to your inner voice and see what it says. Does it offer praise – "well done", "good job", "you look great" – or insults – "you're such an idiot", "why did you say that?", "you always get that wrong"? Listen to your self-talk – would you speak to your friends the way you talk to yourself? If a friend described themselves as a loser, you'd instantly tell them how wrong they were, and talk up their strengths and good qualities. Do the same for yourself – be your own best friend.

44

ENJOY BEING "UNCOOL"

Once you stop crafting your online persona and thinking about trying to impress your friends and followers, you are free to get back in touch with your passions. Don't waste any time worrying that you're not "cool" enough for anyone. When you're not seeing life as potential "content", you may be surprised by what you find you're truly drawn to. Perhaps you're a fan of knitting, old movies and colouring books? Enjoy diving into things that give you real pleasure. Being your authentic self is the coolest thing you can be.

45

FACE YOUR FEARS

Do one thing a day that scares you. In her book *Feel the Fear and Do It Anyway*, Susan Jeffers says that each time we take a step into the unknown we experience fear, but paradoxically the only way to get rid of that fear is to do that thing that scares us. Of course, this could be anything from wearing a colour you usually avoid or tackling an anxiety-inducing task to public speaking, going for a promotion or signing up for a marathon. But perhaps you are also scared of going without social media? After all, it's a social prop, a constant distraction and a way to avoid uncomfortable feelings, not to mention dodging richer, more nuanced one-on-one connection with friends and loved ones. Try facing your fears around giving up social media – you'll feel stronger for it.

46

BE EQUAL

Sometimes people with low self-esteem view other people as more deserving or better than themselves. For instance, after years of comparing yourself with friends and influencers on social media, you might see yourself as less than them (less good-looking, less cool, less entertaining). Try shifting to an "equality mentality", where you are at the same level as other people. When you see yourself as being equal to others, you'll see that they're not better or more deserving than you, only different to you, and your self-confidence will increase.

47

KNOW YOU'RE "GOOD ENOUGH"

The "good enough" movement has recently grown up online in response to the images of perfection that have become currency on social media: the stylish new mum with the clean, beautifully dressed, smiling baby; the athleisure-clad influencer holding her acai bowl covered in a symmetrical arrangement of berries and seeds; the fashionista looking effortlessly chic. It's important to remember that perfection is a dangerous ideal and, in fact, what you're doing or being already is an achievement in itself. Every time social media starts to make you feel inferior to someone or something, remind yourself that you're good enough and that's all you need to be.

48

EMBRACE WHAT MAKES YOU UNIQUE

Self-esteem grows from self-acceptance. That means accepting who you are and not who you think you're supposed to be, i.e. the edited version who gets splashed across social media. You must accept your good qualities as well as your bad ones, because everyone has both. Don't believe all the images you see online – no one is perfect, and if they were, the world would be a boring place. Self-acceptance means learning to love yourself, warts and all. Once you can do that, your confidence will rise and you won't seek validation elsewhere (i.e. by fishing for likes on Instagram).

49

WRITE YOUR POWER LISTS

Write a list of everything that you are thankful for. Then write another list of all the things you are proud of accomplishing. Once your lists are complete, post them on your fridge, on the wall above your desk or by your bathroom mirror – somewhere where you will be reminded of what you have and what you've achieved. Life is full of challenges, some more enjoyable than others, but don't forget how much you've done, how much you're capable of and how strong you are. To put that in context: saying no to social media is a piece of cake!

CURATE POSITIVITY

Taking control of your social media use – tackling the vicious circle of negative emotions, focusing on your offline life, and getting back in touch with your true self – can also involve transforming your experience of social media. Rather than following accounts and people that make you feel edgy and anxious, turn it into a tool for joy, humour and doing good. Remember that the world online doesn't have to be negative. Here are some ways to make it constructive.

50

FOLLOW POSITIVE ACCOUNTS

Keep your eye out for accounts that make you smile, teach you something new and useful, and that inspire you to start new projects – perhaps your favourite charities or causes have Instagram accounts, Facebook pages or groups, or Twitter feeds? Or do you enjoy vintage photos, pictures of cute animals or great food shots? Some meme accounts can provide an instant laugh. If you want something more profound, follow a therapist with important insights into mental and emotional health. Motivational quote accounts are also great for boosting your mood and making you think.

51

UNFOLLOW THE NEGATIVE

Get spring-cleaning! It doesn't matter if they're a close friend – if their account makes you feel bad, unfollow them or delete them as a friend. If you'd rather be more subtle about it, mute them on Instagram and Twitter, meaning their posts won't appear in your feed but they won't know about it, and hide them on Facebook. Remove those accounts that make you feel inferior, envious, annoyed or just leave you feeling a bit off. The political ranter, the humble bragger, the smug green-juicer, the bore – they can all go. You don't need to give your attention to anything that brings you down.

52

DON'T FEED THE TROLLS

Trolling and cyberbullying are a horrible fact of life on social media. If you share your thoughts in a public forum, other people will inevitably have an opinion. If anyone posts anything rude or insulting on your feeds, don't reply to them or get caught in an argument – discussions in social media comments escalate quickly and are rarely resolved well. However, if you're being bullied, tell someone (a friend, parents, tutors or even an employer), and if you're a victim of abuse, you must report the accounts and block the poster.

53

SPREAD JOY

Yes, some people boast on social media, but others are just sharing good news or achievements they are proud of. They may have run a marathon, which is a huge feat, or passed a driving test or been given a new job. Or perhaps they're volunteering for a charity or spreading the word about a worthy cause. They might be announcing a life milestone – an engagement or pregnancy. If you see a friend doing something great, leave a comment and be supportive. If you see a post that you love, feel free to like it. If they look and sound happy in their post, leave them a note or a fitting emoji. Spreading joy can make you feel happy too.

54

IMPROVE YOUR CHOICES

Expose yourself to new, positive Instagram accounts and Facebook posts by influencing your algorithms. Every time you follow a specific kind of account on Instagram, a fashion one, for instance, it will suggest more fashion accounts for you to follow. So, click on the "search" button at the bottom of your screen, scroll through and choose a range of different accounts being suggested to you. This will increase the variety recommended to you in the future. On Facebook, look at your settings – change your news feed from "top stories" (i.e. the ones with the most engagement) to "most recent", and weed through your feed, putting regular posters on "snooze" for 30 days, to mix up what you see.

55

FIND YOUR TRIBES

One of the admirable things about social media is the way it provides a place for like-minded individuals or professional communities. If you're a passionate owner of a VW Camper Van, joining a group filled with people who share your interests – and who could help you with any problems related to your vehicle – will be both enjoyable and useful. New mothers can find support and understanding, while in remote villages online groups can bring people together in a different way. Equally, there are professional groups on Facebook that are invaluable for networking and sharing information. Just make sure these groups are run by administrators who aren't afraid to shut down conversation if members break the rules of civility and politeness.

56

MUTE HASHTAGS

Twitter offers users the chance to mute hashtags that have negative connotations, ensuring that any posts featuring that hashtag won't appear in your notifications tab, push notifications, SMSs, email notifications or home timeline. So banish from your feed any trigger words or terms that make you feel sad, anxious or angry. This could range from #weightloss or #thinspo to the hashtags associated with a news story you find distressing. On a lighter note, it can also help you avoid spoilers about your favourite show by muting its title and other hashtags associated with it so you can watch it in your own time. Go to Settings > Notifications > Muted > Muted Words > tap the "+" and add any words you like.

57

BE HONEST

Think carefully about what you post on social media and how it will come across, and, whatever you post, make sure it's honest. For instance, try giving up photo-enhancing features on your devices and pledge to make your snaps more creative and authentic. This will fire up your imagination and may give you a sense of achievement too, in creating something that thought and effort have gone into and that other people will enjoy. Your accounts can be places of honesty, acceptance and positivity – for both you and your friends and followers.

58

DON'T LURK

Active members of social media are happier than passive lurkers. A University of Copenhagen study warns about the impact of "lurking" – passively scrolling, watching other people's lives – which can lower your mood. However, actively engaging in conversation and connecting with people makes social media a happier experience. So make a positive decision to be an engaged follower or friend. Like and comment on people's posts as you see fit. You could even give yourself a target of writing five comments per visit to your feeds – it will keep you on track and stop yourself from mindlessly scrolling. But if you find yourself slipping into your old passive habits, log off.

59

INSPIRATION v. COMPARISON

Reframe the way you observe other people's posts. When friends inevitably do post pictures from their dream holiday or share their achievements, don't take it personally. After all, someone else's success doesn't diminish your own. Don't compare your life with theirs. In fact, see their success as inspiration. If *they* can do that triathlon, why not you? A friend who's had their book published – wow. What insight can they give you to help with your own writing project? That friend enjoying a Bali beach holiday? Great! Now you have a source of information for your long-planned Indonesian trip. Rather than using social media to dwell on how much your life is lacking, see it as a vehicle to help you work toward your goals.

STAY CONNECTED

True connection with friends, family and your fellow humans needs to be done the old-fashioned way – in person or speaking over the phone. No matter how many times you like someone's photo, it will create no more intimacy than if you hadn't seen anything about them during the same period of time. Get ready for some real-time interaction – it will make you feel connected in a whole new way.

60

CALL FRIENDS

The next time you want to talk or make an arrangement with a friend, you might be tempted to start tapping in Facebook Messenger or to message them on Instagram. Stop right there! Get on the phone and call them. Talking to friends and family on the phone will bring a whole new dynamic to all your social interactions. Just think – there's no chance of misreading something that someone has said, and you can make a plan in one 5-minute call rather than stringing it out over an hour of messaging while you're both doing other things. It's also harder to multitask when you're in conversation, giving you greater focus on the chat in hand. It's a deeper, richer experience than DM-ing.

61

DO WHAT YOU LOVE

Pursue a hobby like a dance class, an art class or a running group. You'll be doing something that interests you, expanding your horizons and probably meeting new people. Invite some friends to join you to make it even more sociable. There's the added advantage that while you're busy learning the steps to Beyoncé's "Single Ladies" dance, or improving your 5K speed at your local Parkrun, you won't have time to look at your phone – which should be safely tucked away in your bag.

62

HAVE FRIENDS ROUND

Throw a dinner party – light some candles and cook three courses for a group of friends, or just get your best mate over to eat a bowl of cereal together. The act of planning the event, as well as the time spent chatting, will be so enjoyable you won't even think about social media. Plus the conversation will be better and funnier than anything you could do together on social media. Make sure your guests understand that phones are to be left in their bags.

63

VOLUNTEER

There's little that will give your life deeper meaning and connect you to new people like volunteering. Hand out leaflets for a charity, volunteer to keep elderly people company at home or join a litter-picking walk. Choose something that's personal to you, and feel free to post on social media once you've finished the session for the day – after all, sharing a positive message and raising awareness among your friends and followers is important, and one of the upsides of social media.

64

SMALL TALK CAN BECOME BIG TALK

If you find making conversation with strangers or acquaintances a challenge, or you dread being "stuck" next to someone at a dinner party, try thinking about it differently, especially since looking at your phone at a party or event is not only antisocial but rude. Ask yourself: "what can I learn from them?" A more open mindset can transform an encounter into an interesting experience. Remember that everyone you will ever meet knows something you don't.

65

START CONVERSATIONS

When you're not staring at your phone you'll realize how many people you pass every day. Most of us operate in public in a state of self-imposed isolation, but why not end that and exchange a passing word with them? Research suggests that we may underestimate the positive impact of connecting with people for our own and others' well-being. Exchanging a few brief words with people you encounter during your day may leave you feeling happier than you might think. Tell a sales assistant you like her nail colour, chat to the postman, ask the newsagent about the shop's cat or give a tourist directions.

66

SAY "YES" TO SPONTANEITY

When someone invites you to something new, just say yes. Even if you don't feel like it, it's raining outside, or you've never done karaoke before. You might be with old friends, or newer pals, but you're exposing yourself to new things, new people and new conversations. And the people around you will love your positive mental attitude. Don't overcommit yourself – you've read about the dangers of trying to be everywhere at once in an effort to beat FOMO – but do ask yourself why you instinctively want to reject an invite. Has dependency on social media made your IRL social skills a bit rusty? Is it just easier to chat online or look at someone's feed rather than have a conversation? It's time to break out of that social media comfort zone.

67

MAKE PEOPLE FEEL GOOD

Do you use social media as an emotional prop? Maybe a quick exchange with someone online makes you feel seen and heard, so perhaps you spend more time on your accounts to try to get that same validation, often with diminishing returns? It's time for a reminder that your community isn't just online – it's all around you. Try this exercise: every day, do something nice for, or say something nice to, two strangers. You could give a genuine compliment, or hold a door open for a parent struggling with a buggy. Flash a real smile to someone who looks like they need it. This will change your mindset, helping you to see the world around you as welcoming, full of positive interaction and possible connection.

68

GET A DUMBPHONE

You can stay connected with your loved ones without being sucked into social media with what's known as a dumbphone – the kinds of phones people used to have before the iPhone was launched in 2007. Old-fashioned flip phones are newly popular, as are basic mobiles with small screens and button keypads. These models strip back the mobile experience to the essentials: you can make calls, text and send photos, but there's no internet. The best thing? You can talk to anyone you like, for as long as you like, because the biggest advantage of dumbphones is the battery life – up to three weeks per charge.

69

YOUR NEW DM RULES

Do you find that you spend so much time messaging your friends and family that by the time you see them you've covered most of what you want to say? Create a new rule in your social circle and among your loved ones around DMs. Limit your communication on Facebook Messenger, for instance, to simply making plans – the wheres and whens of a meet-up. Do not ask each other about anything personal and save all your life news for when you see each other face to face. This will encourage you to arrange catch-ups in person, and prevent you from diving into your DMs for your social fix (see more on the new social etiquette on page 111).

MOOD BOOSTERS

If you still feel trapped in a negative cycle of social media use, or have indeed managed to cut down your use but feel low without your social media prop, there are practical ways to clear your head, cheer yourself up and help you feel more centred. Move your body, have a moment of mindfulness or stimulate your senses. Don't be tempted to turn back to social media as a coping mechanism or distraction – you have a much bigger emotional and social toolkit now.

70

GO OUTSIDE

Experts say that stressful, engrossing activity stimulates our sympathetic nervous system, which leads to feeling tired but wired. So those hours on social media, which may seem harmless, are impacting on your well-being. Fortunately there's an antidote: a moment away from your screen, and getting some sunlight and fresh air. Nature triggers our parasympathetic nervous system, which is responsible for the restore and rest areas of our brain – vital to allow us to relax and enjoy a good night's sleep.

71

GO FOR A RUN

Running is great for heart health and releasing endorphins, but brain scans also show that it has a similar effect on the brain as meditation. In the middle of a run, you are very present, in tune with your body and focusing on your breathing – all of which is the opposite of using social media, where your attention is flicking from one thing to the next. So running could transform your mood as well as increase your fitness. But if you're still in need of an online boost, there are several apps that track fitness and allow you to invite other running friends to join challenges, enabling you to use social media in a positive way.

72

TRY YOGA

Creating a satisfying life away from social media involves embracing new activities. Yoga increases strength, flexibility and feelings of calm – no wonder it's been used in the treatment of anxiety conditions, depression and insomnia. It can lower the stress hormone cortisol and reduce your heart rate and blood pressure. Add to that the feeling of achievement when you finally hold a pose for the first time. Following YouTube star Yoga with Adriene (youtube.com/user/yogawithadriene) at home is a great place to start, but going to a class – perhaps with a friend – will get you out and among new people. Keep a diary or download a yoga-tracking app to focus on your progress – it'll help you take your mind off what's going on online.

73

LISTEN TO MUSIC

When you're away from social media do you feel antsy, on edge and tempted to dive back in and find out what you've missed? This is where music comes in. It's proven to change our emotional state – slow, calming songs have a chill-out effect, while faster, louder pieces will ramp us up. Research has found that music apparently activates the brain structures and neurochemical systems associated with positive mood, emotion regulation, memory and attention. Make a Spotify playlist that's full of your favourite uplifting, toe-tapping music. These should be the tracks that have happy associations and always put a smile on your face. No sad songs here! Who needs to turn to their feeds for stimulation when you've got a veritable disco on tap wherever you go?

74

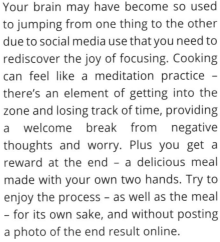

GET COOKING

Your brain may have become so used to jumping from one thing to the other due to social media use that you need to rediscover the joy of focusing. Cooking can feel like a meditation practice – there's an element of getting into the zone and losing track of time, providing a welcome break from negative thoughts and worry. Plus you get a reward at the end – a delicious meal made with your own two hands. Try to enjoy the process – as well as the meal – for its own sake, and without posting a photo of the end result online.

75

TIDY UP

Now that you've got your social media habit under control, you should have more time on your hands to create the kind of life you want to live. Ask yourself: "do I feel weighed down by stuff?" Clutter-clearing can seem daunting but the results are worth the effort. Go through your wardrobe and create four piles of clothes: to keep, for the bin/recycling, for charity and for mending. Go through storage boxes or bags of belongings and decide what to keep, donate, bin or recycle. Throw away or recycle out-of-date beauty products. You'll feel physically lighter once your clear-out is done.

76

BREATHE YOURSELF BETTER

When you feel the urge to pick up your phone for a quick look at your social media accounts, take a breath – literally. Try a calming breathing technique that helps to tackle stress. Place one hand on your belly and the other on your chest. Take a deep breath in through your nose, making sure that your diaphragm (your stomach, not your chest) inflates. Slowly exhale. According to experts, taking six to ten slow, deep breaths per minute for 10 minutes every day can lower your heart rate and blood pressure. If it doesn't come naturally at first, just keep practising.

77

HAVE A BOOGIE

Dancing is not only good for the body, but it has a powerful effect on the brain because when we dance our brain releases feel-good endorphins. Music and dance activate the sensory and motor circuits of our brain as well as the pleasure centres. When we move with the beat, these positive effects are amplified. These benefits can be enjoyed at home alone as you cut a rug to your favourite song, but you can also turn dancing into a social activity, so arrange a night of dancing with friends or head to a dance class at the gym.

78

HUG SOMEONE

Have you touched anyone today? Physical connection releases oxytocin, a hormone produced by the hypothalamus that gives us a warm feeling. It's a sensation that can't be prompted by hunching over our phones scrolling endlessly through our social media feeds. Hugging can make you feel less stressed and even have long-term health benefits. If you're in a relationship, or have family close at hand, make an effort to be more tactile with them. If you're single, try greeting good friends with a squeeze (make sure they're fond of hugging first though).

79

WATCH YOUR BODY LANGUAGE

Facing life without the protective bubble of social media can be intimidating – you may be so used to having your phone in your hand and posting your every move online, not to mention watching everyone else's. So when you're feeling vulnerable and you need an extra dose of IRL confidence, try this exercise. Give yourself a mental body scan, assessing your posture and stance. If you're sitting down, lower your shoulders, straighten your back and plant your feet squarely on the floor. If standing, set your feet shoulder width apart and imagine that your head is a balloon and your back is a piece of string. Forget that your phone is within reach. Simply sit or stand tall – don't cower or hunch – and you'll feel ready to take on anything.

KEEPING IT UP

Congratulations for gaining control over your social media use and getting important perspective on your habit. You may be wondering what to do now and there's no reason why you can't continue on social media in a healthy, empowered way. Here are some tips to keep you on track and even turn your social media use into a force for good.

80

SLOW DOWN

You may be used to sharing everything on your accounts, whether it's doing an Instagram story on your breakfast or posting a picture of your new shoes. But instead of that continuous oversharing, try sharing half of what you'd usually post and see how you feel. You will feel liberated knowing that you can enjoy your day-to-day activities without worrying about taking photos and videos to create content for your account. However, you will still be posting enough to feel that you are engaging with your friends on social media.

81

ASK WHY

Before you post something, think about what you want to achieve by posting it. Question your motivation, and then think about how your followers and friends might respond to it. Do you want their validation? Are you looking for attention? Or do you in fact want to achieve something specific, such as raise money for charity? If it's the former, think again about posting and do something that will give you a genuine boost instead. But if it's the latter, go right ahead.

82

BE PURPOSEFUL

Before you click on to your accounts, think about how you will spend your time on social media – have a purpose. If you have a plan in place you are less likely to fall into the trap of mindless scrolling. Perhaps you want to wish someone a happy birthday, or share an article, or you feel like having a 5-minute break from work. Set a timer if you need to, or write a list of the tasks you want to tick off, then once you've completed what you planned to do, log out.

83

GIVE YOURSELF SCROLL TIME

Everyone's allowed to relax, so why not build social media scrolling time into your day? This will be a short period of time – one daily slot of half an hour, or two slots of 15 minutes – where you can dive into your accounts and gaze at posts, pictures and memes. By creating specific periods in your day – scheduled in your diary if you're really organized – you are stopping yourself from doing it more frequently throughout the day and undoing all the amazing work you've done on changing your social media habits.

84

TRACK YOUR MOOD

Download a mood tracker app or buy a mood tracker journal to start monitoring how social media affects your emotions. Be careful to track your emotions when you're offline as well as online. This can become a powerful tool for days that have been taken up by social media but which have left you feeling low. Tracking your emotional response to social media is particularly useful as it is increasingly linked with feelings of unhappiness. In a 2018 survey of 1,000 people described as Generation Z, 41 per cent stated that social media platforms made them feel depressed, sad or anxious, while more than a third said they were leaving social media for good. Become more aware of how social media affects you so you can regulate your usage.

85

FEEL GOOD FIRST

Attitude is important, especially when you engage with social media. Before you click on Facebook, for instance, stop and ask yourself how you're feeling. Are you bitter? Frustrated? Bored? If you are, you're likely to view posts and photos through that lens, feeling jealous and twitchy at glimpses of other lives. If you're in a cheery mood, however, you'll enjoy those updates from other people's worlds. So next time you start to log in to your accounts, do a quick mood audit: are you in the right headspace for social media? If you're feeling good, your social media session will feel good, so go ahead.

86

CHANGE THE CONVERSATION

Everyone has the ability to talk about and to encourage and focus on positive topics on their feeds. Before posting anything, Upworthy co-founder Peter Koechley asks himself: "If a million people see this, will it make the world a better place?" This can apply to anything you do. It's in your power to share positive messages, and to like and comment warmly on other people's feeds. So rather than allowing social media to discourage you, use it to encourage others.

87

BECOME PHUB AWARE

Phone snubbing (ignoring other people by staring at your phone) is such a common phenomenon that it has its own term, "phubbing". Quite simply, it's rude. But do you find yourself doing it when you've got company? It's easy to do – one minute you're looking something up to show a friend, and the next, you've quickly read some DMs and are having a sneaky scroll through Instagram. When you're socializing, answering an urgent text or taking a selfie or photo to capture the moment is normal, but ignoring people and responding to every ping and vibration from your device is bad manners. The best way to avoid phubbing is to put your phone away during social events – and keep it there.

88

STAY TRUE TO YOURSELF

If you're comfortable being your true, authentic self IRL then make sure you maintain that authenticity on social media. This means not trying to be perfect or not attempting to be someone you're not online. When you're authentic it's easy to decide what to share on your feeds because those posts, pictures and comments are an extension of yourself – social media won't be a performance. An added bonus is that your friends and family will recognize the person they see posting on Instagram, for instance, as the same person they know offline.

89

CREATE LINKS

By now you know how comparing yourself with other people just makes you unhappy in the long run. However, making genuine connections with others can enhance overall well-being. The next time you're on social media, see how you can create links with other people – message an old friend or an elderly relative. Is a friend having a hard time? Send them something that will brighten their day.

TAKING IT FURTHER

Hopefully you have a very different view of social media now. *You* are in charge, and you're the one who makes the choice about when to dip in and out of it – and how to use social media to enhance your life. You've put effort and passion into your life offline, and you have the tools to boost your well-being, change your perspective and give your life meaning. So how can you continue the great work you've started? Here are some ideas.

DETOX WEEKEND

Consider steering clear of social media for an entire weekend. You can choose the exact times, but your detox could start at 6.30 p.m. on Friday evening and end 48 hours later. Or why not push through until 9 a.m. on Monday morning? Detox during a busy weekend at home when you have a full schedule or let it coincide with a break from the norm – a camping trip, for instance. If you're out in nature, be fully present in it and don't let your feeds distract you – plus it's likely you won't have a great signal, so this is a good way to stay offline without temptations. You could log back in again once you're home.

91

SET A BUDGET

We've already talked about setting time limits on social media use, but now you're ready to take the idea further by being super disciplined every day. Give yourself a daily social media "budget", for example 30 minutes a day. You could blow your budget in one go, or measure the time spent on all of your social sessions throughout the day, to make sure you're not breaching your daily social media budget. Those snatched interludes on your favourite feeds will be more focused – and because they're limited, more enjoyable.

92

DEACTIVATE YOUR ACCOUNTS

Taking your accounts off the table could be the most freeing thing to do. Just remember that deactivating isn't the same thing as deleting (when you lose your photos, videos and memories). On Facebook go to Settings > General > Your Facebook information > Deactivation and deletion and type in your password. For Instagram, log in from a mobile browser or on a computer (not the app), click "Edit Profile", select "temporarily disable my account" and enter your password to deactivate. For Twitter, click Settings > Privacy > Account > Deactivate Your Account > Deactivate @username. But don't worry if you're struggling to go cold turkey – you have at least 30 days to change your mind and restore your accounts.

93

BOOK A BLACKOUT

Organize a social media blackout with a group of friends. You can all discuss the specific terms – it could be over an agreed period of time, let's say a typical week, or during a group activity such as a weekend getaway. Essentially, you will all agree not to engage with your social media feeds during that time – so no posts, comments or likes. To take it further, you could deactivate your accounts together. It will be much easier if you're all in it together as it will be a shared challenge and it could change the way you interact with each other in surprising ways.

94

MAKE YOUR PHONE LESS USEFUL

Before we had smartphones tempting us with distractions including music, games and the infinite scroll of social media, we had separate gadgets, books and maps. The result is that we've become completely helpless without our phones in our hands. So go back in time by investing in a landline phone, a stereo and a watch. Buy physical books, subscribe to newspapers and magazines, and get hold of an A–Z map – these items may feel ancient, but you'll never be at the mercy of mobile data and Wi-Fi again to perform life's daily tasks and pleasures, or to find where you're meant to be going. Plus, the less cause you have to reach for your phone, the fewer times you'll be tempted to hop on to Facebook and the like.

95

STORE MEMORIES

You may still be clinging to your social media accounts because they're packed with your favourite photos and memories. Set aside time to download photos and chats so you have them stored on your computer instead. On Facebook, click on "options" at the bottom of the photo and click "download" (or "save" if you are using the app). Or select what you'd like to download (messages, chats, your data) by clicking Settings > Your Facebook information > Download your information. On Instagram, click "security" and "download data". On Twitter, tap Settings > Privacy > Account > Your Twitter data > Download an archive of your data. Social media will become a lot less appealing when you don't need it to see your old snaps.

96

TAKE DIGITAL SABBATHS

You've given yourself the odd weekend off social media, but now you're ready for a weekly internet-free day. Choose your day of rest – for instance, all day Sunday, or Friday 6 p.m. to Saturday 6 p.m. – and then shut all your devices down. Feel free to post on your feeds letting your friends and followers know that you're "going dark" for a day then log off from your computer and, if it's a laptop, put it somewhere out of sight. Do the same with your phone – turn it off and stow it in a drawer where you won't be able to see it. Share your landline number with close friends and family in case there's an emergency. Enjoy the freedom that comes with not being tethered to any devices for the day – you'll be doing it again next week.

97

MAKE SOCIAL OCCASIONS PHONELESS

The next time you have friends over, ask all your guests to put their phones in a bag when they arrive and only collect them when they leave. If it's an emergency, people can reach you on your landline. You'll be in good company – Yondr has created phone pouches that can be locked by a concert or comedy club venue until the show is over, creating a phone-free environment. Artists including Haim and Chris Rock have used it to keep live audiences engaged and to try out new material without having it uploaded to YouTube.

98

THE NEW WAYS TO RSVP

The next time you organize an event, take your planning off social media – not everyone is on Facebook or will see your invite notification anyway. If you're arranging a party, try emailing or sending invitations via Paperless Post (paperlesspost.com) – guests will be more likely to see your invitation and you won't be constantly drawn into Facebook after logging in to check your guests' attendance. If you're getting a small group together, use Doodle (doodle.com) or Calendly (calendly.com) to quickly choose an optimum date.

99

DO NOT DISTURB

This is about to become your new favourite smartphone tool. Find "Do Not Disturb" on iPhone under "Settings" or in Android tap Settings > Sounds > Do not disturb. Use this setting for periods when you don't want to be interrupted, such as in meetings, formal events or at night. The function stops notifications, alerts and calls from making any noise, vibration or lighting up the screen when it's locked. Your alarms will still go off, you can select override for calls from specific contacts so they will always ring through and you can opt to have repeated calls ring through so you won't miss someone trying to reach you urgently.

100

HAND OVER YOUR PHONE

If you still find it hard to keep away from social media even when you've tried all the other tips in this book, try handing your phone over to your partner, a parent, a close friend or someone you trust. They will look after your device and will only give it back to you when you ask for it. The caveat should be that you can't ask for it for at least half a day. Good luck!

CONCLUSION

Whatever your reasons for changing the way you interact with social media, hopefully this book has been helpful and has given you a greater awareness of why you use social media and its effect on you.

The key message is to build up resilience, contentment and connection in real life. When you invest in a supportive community of friends and family, you won't feel lonely and seek digital connection on social media as a substitute. And when you have a routine filled with fresh air, exercise, laughter, conversation and hobbies, you have everything you need to feel validated and content in the world around you. You won't be drawn into social media for a false sense of affirmation.

Don't be too hard on yourself if you still find yourself falling into a Facebook or Snapchat black hole. Changing habits is a long-term process and slipping up is natural – it certainly doesn't mean you've "failed". Keep using the steps in this book to keep you on track and remind yourself of why you've made this commitment to limit your social media use.

Social media is fun, informative and can be a force for good, as long as it's part of a rich, multidimensional life. Enjoy the journey!

If you're interested in finding out more about our books, find us on Facebook at **Summersdale Publishers** and follow us on Twitter at **@Summersdale**.

www.summersdale.com

IMAGE CREDITS

Brain/bulb icon © maglyvi/Shutterstock.com
Chevrons © Kirill Mlayshev/Shutterstock.com
Down arrow icon © ibrandify gallery/Shutterstock.com
Heart icon © Webicon/Shutterstock.com
No phone icon © Kaissa/Shutterstock.com
Stopwatch icon © Rashad Ashur/Shutterstock.com
p.6 © andrerosi/Shutterstock.com
p.7 © Avector/Shutterstock.com
p.8 © vladwel/Shutterstock.com
p.9 © Alex Gontar/Shutterstock.com
p.10 © M-vector/Shutterstock.com
p.11 © Z-art/Shutterstock.com
p.12 © StarGraphic/Shutterstock.com
p.13 © vladwel/Shutterstock.com
p.14 © StarGraphic/Shutterstock.com
p.15 © Anna Frajtova/Shutterstock.com